Lerner SPORTS

ALL-STAR SMACKDOWN

AARON DONALD VS. REGGIE WHITE

WHO WOULD WIN?

DAVID STABLER

Lerner Publications ◆ Minneapolis

Copyright © 2024 by Lerner Publishing Group, Inc.

All rights reserved. International copyright secured. No part of this book may be reproduced, stored in a retrieval system, or transmitted in any form or by any means—electronic, mechanical, photocopying, recording, or otherwise—without the prior written permission of Lerner Publishing Group, Inc., except for the inclusion of brief quotations in an acknowledged review.

Lerner Publications Company
An imprint of Lerner Publishing Group, Inc.
241 First Avenue North
Minneapolis, MN 55401 USA

For reading levels and more information, look up this title at www.lernerbooks.com.

Main body text set in Aptifer Sans LT Pro.
Typeface provided by Linotype AG.

Library of Congress Cataloging-in-Publication Data

Names: Stabler, David, author.
Title: Aaron Donald vs. Reggie White : who would win? / David Stabler.
Description: Minneapolis, MN : Lerner Publications, [2024] | Series: All-star smackdown (Lerner sports) | Includes bibliographical references and index. | Audience: Ages 7–11 | Audience: Grades 2–3 | Summary: "Defensive tackle Aaron Donald and defensive tackle and end Reggie White are fast, powerful football stars. Dive into their careers side by side to discover which player is best"—Provided by publisher.
Identifiers: LCCN 2022042973 (print) | LCCN 2022042974 (ebook) | ISBN 9781728490861 (library binding) | ISBN 9798765602447 (paperback) | ISBN 9781728495705 (ebook)
Subjects: LCSH: Donald, Aaron, 1991– —Juvenile literature. | White, Reggie,—Juvenile literature. | Football players—United States—Biography—Juvenile literature. | Football—Defense—Juvenile literature.
Classification: LCC GV939.D646 S73 2024 (print) | LCC GV939.D646 (ebook) | DDC 796.33092 [B]—dc23/eng/20220916

LC record available at https://lccn.loc.gov/2022042973
LC ebook record available at https://lccn.loc.gov/2022042974

Manufactured in the United States of America
4-1011322-51035-5/17/2024

TABLE OF CONTENTS

Introduction
Super Bowl Superstars 4

Chapter 1
Road to the NFL 8

Chapter 2
Great Moments 12

Chapter 3
Tackling by the Numbers 18

Chapter 4
And the Winner Is 24

Smackdown Breakdown. 28
Glossary. 30
Learn More 31
Index 32

Reggie White

INTRODUCTION
SUPER BOWL SUPERSTARS

Things weren't looking good for the Green Bay Packers after the first quarter of the 1997 Super Bowl. The New England Patriots led the game 14–10. But the Packers were not finished. Their offense exploded in the second quarter to take a 27–14 halftime lead.

Fast Facts

- Reggie White joined the Pro Football Hall of Fame in 2006.
- White was the NFL's all-time leader with 198 sacks when he retired.
- Aaron Donald has won National Football League (NFL) Defensive Player of the Year three times.
- Donald made the Pro Bowl, the NFL's all-star game, in each of his first nine seasons.

New England attempted a comeback in the second half. But Reggie White took over for the Packers. Green Bay's star defensive end sacked Patriots quarterback Drew Bledsoe twice in a row to stop them. White added one more sack late in the fourth quarter to clinch the game. With three sacks, he set a new NFL record for sacks in a Super Bowl game. The Packers took home their first championship in 29 years.

Aaron Donald

    Twenty-five years later, Los Angeles Rams defensive tackle Aaron Donald made his mark on the big game. In the 2022 Super Bowl, Donald chased Cincinnati Bengals quarterback Joe Burrow all game. The Rams built up a slim 23–20 lead. Late in the fourth quarter, Cincinnati had the ball with a chance to win. But Donald sacked Burrow with less than a minute left to play. Donald's second sack of the game sealed LA's victory. The Rams won their first Super Bowl in 22 years.

    Reggie White and Aaron Donald star in sacking the quarterback. They both made big impacts by leading their teams to Super Bowl wins. But which of these defensive linemen is truly the greatest of all time? We're about to find out. Let the smackdown begin!

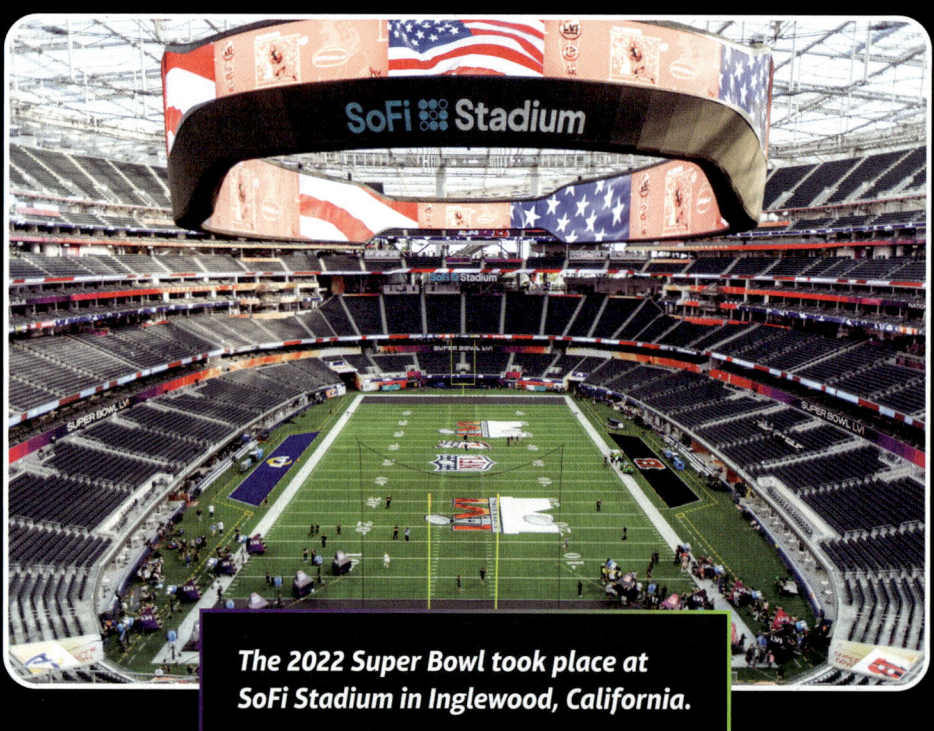

The 2022 Super Bowl took place at SoFi Stadium in Inglewood, California.

Aaron Donald grabs Cincinnati Bengals quarterback Joe Burrow and drags him to the ground near the end of the 2022 Super Bowl.

CHAPTER 1

Reggie White (right) and his University of Tennessee teammates try to stop the Georgia Bulldogs from scoring.

ROAD TO THE NFL

Reggie White was born on December 19, 1961, in Chattanooga, Tennessee. When he was 12, he told his mother that he wanted to be two things when he grew up: a football player and a minister. A minister is a Christian religious leader.

White played football at Howard High School. In his final year, he recorded 140 tackles and 10 sacks. He was an All-American, one of the best high school players in the United

States. He also achieved his other goal by becoming a minister at 17.

When he graduated, White was the top high school football prospect in Tennessee. He received a scholarship to play at the University of Tennessee. In four years, he set a school record with 32 sacks and won many awards.

White, in his University of Tennessee uniform, with head coach Johnny Majors

White could have jumped straight to the NFL. But he chose to play in a new professional football league, the United States Football League. After two seasons with the Memphis Showboats, White joined the NFL's Philadelphia Eagles in 1985.

Aaron Donald followed a similar path to the NFL. Born on May 23, 1991, he grew up in Pittsburgh, Pennsylvania. By 14, he was working out for nearly two hours a day in a basement gym his father built. The workouts helped Donald develop strength and speed to excel as a defensive lineman at Penn Hills High School.

Donald (top) sacks the quarterback during a 2013 college game against Georgia Tech.

CONSIDER THIS

With his background as a religious leader, Reggie White's nickname was the Minister of Defense. Aaron Donald's nickname is The Terminator for his strength and fierce play.

Like Reggie White, Aaron Donald also played college football in his home state. Donald attended the University of Pittsburgh. In four years, he racked up 29.5 sacks, including 11 sacks in his last season. The Rams selected Donald with the 13th overall pick in the 2014 NFL Draft.

Donald (center) uses his strength and speed to rush the quarterback during his first season with the Rams.

CHAPTER 2

Reggie White (right) pushes a Cleveland Browns blocker. White played for the Eagles from 1985 to 1992.

GREAT MOMENTS

Reggie White made an impact in his very first NFL game. He recorded 10 tackles and sacked the New York Giants quarterback 2.5 times as the new Eagles defensive end. The home crowd in Philadelphia, Pennsylvania, was chanting his name by the end of the game.

For the season, White collected 13 total sacks and 100 tackles. He won the NFL Defensive Rookie of the Year award.

White was even better the next season. He recorded four sacks in a game twice—once against the St. Louis Cardinals and once against the Los Angeles Raiders.

White lines up for the next play in a 1987 game. He recorded 21 sacks that season, the most of his career.

White fights off a blocker during the 1997 Super Bowl. He helped Green Bay beat the New England Patriots 35–21.

In a 1987 game against Washington, White made one of the most amazing defensive plays in NFL history. He swooped in on Washington quarterback Doug Williams, stole the ball out of his hands, and ran 70 yards for a touchdown. Even though he weighed about 285 pounds (129 kg), White could run faster than many smaller players. No one could catch him as he sped into the end zone.

After eight seasons in Philadelphia, White signed with the Green Bay Packers in 1993. With his history of NFL success, many people expected White to play well and become a team leader with the Packers. He lived up to the hype and led Green Bay to a Super Bowl championship in his fourth year with the team.

Aaron Donald also had a standout rookie season. He made four tackles in his first game and finished the year with 48 tackles and nine sacks. He won the NFL Defensive Rookie of the Year award. Donald also made the Pro Bowl for the first time. He has been a Pro Bowl player every year of his NFL career.

Donald (right) tackles a Baltimore Ravens running back. No matter who has the ball, Donald can take them down.

In his fourth season with the Rams, Donald had one of the most outstanding months in NFL history. He recorded a sack in four straight games and forced a fumble in three of them. Donald had one of his best games ever later that season. He recorded five tackles, three sacks, and forced another fumble in a 42–7 win over the Seattle Seahawks.

Donald has stayed with the Rams throughout his NFL career. His loyalty to the team paid off in 2022 when the Rams roared through the NFC playoffs. Donald was at his best in the NFC Championship Game. He rushed San Francisco 49ers quarterback Jimmy Garoppolo all game, including on an important play in the fourth quarter. Donald broke through the offensive line and chased Garoppolo. Donald forced Garoppolo to make a bad throw that became a game-sealing interception. The Rams won 20–17 to advance to the Super Bowl.

CONSIDER THIS

Though he didn't start weight training until his fifth NFL season, Reggie White could bench press 425 pounds (193 kg). Aaron Donald is even stronger and can bench 500 pounds (227 kg).

Donald grabs Jimmy Garoppolo during the 2022 NFC Championship Game. Garoppolo avoided the sack by throwing the ball, but his pass was intercepted.

CHAPTER 3

Aaron Donald has averaged more than 11 sacks per season in his NFL career.

TACKLING BY THE NUMBERS

Reggie White and Aaron Donald are both big-game defensive linemen who play their best when their teams need them most. White made the playoffs 10 times in 15 NFL seasons and won one Super Bowl. Donald has made the playoffs four times in eight NFL seasons and also won one Super Bowl. If he plays as long as White did, he is sure to add more playoffs and maybe another Super Bowl title or two.

One way to measure a player's greatness is by the number of times he makes the Pro Bowl. The Minister of Defense comes out ahead with 13 total Pro Bowls to Aaron Donald's nine. But Donald still has several seasons left to close the gap between them.

White (right) tries to get around a blocker during the 1996 Pro Bowl in Honolulu, Hawaii.

White leaps over a Carolina Panthers player during a playoff game in 1997.

What do the stats say? Reggie White recorded 1,111 career tackles and 198 sacks. He led the league in sacks twice and had 12 seasons with ten or more sacks, an NFL record at the time. When he retired in 2000, White was the NFL's all-time sacks leader. He also forced 33 fumbles and made three interceptions in his career. White was a two-time NFL Defensive Player of the Year. He joined the Pro Football Hall of Fame in 2006. In 2019, he was selected for the NFL 100 All-Time Team—a list of the 100 best players in NFL history.

White's wife (left) and son (right) reveal a statue of White's likeness at the Pro Football Hall of Fame in 2006.

The list celebrated the league's 100th anniversary. Aaron Donald had played in just over half the number of games Reggie White did by the end of the 2022 season.

If a quarterback doesn't notice Donald rushing toward them, the result is often a sack and a fumble.

But Donald's stats are also impressive. He had 490 tackles and recorded 103 sacks. And he had forced 24 fumbles and recovered seven of them. He was a three-time NFL Defensive Player of the Year. Experts predict he will join White in the Pro Football Hall of Fame when he retires.

Donald holds the 2017 NFL Defensive Player of the Year award at a ceremony in Minnesota.

CONSIDER THIS

In addition to playing football, White appeared in a couple of pro wrestling matches. In his spare time, Donald has tried acting and appeared on a TV show in 2019.

CHAPTER 4

Donald celebrates a big play with a teammate at the 2022 Super Bowl.

AND THE WINNER IS

Who is the winner of this all-star smackdown? That's for you to decide. Both players are all-time great defensive linemen. There is no right or wrong answer. Everybody has their own opinion. That's part of the fun of being a sports fan. Who do you think is best? Here are some more things to consider.

Reggie White currently has the edge in stats. But the story is not complete. Donald may end up with as many or more sacks and tackles as White had. But Donald may decide to retire before he equals White's totals.

Donald warms up before a game in 2022. He works hard to stay strong and healthy for his team.

When White retired, many fans considered him the all-time greatest defensive end in NFL history. He held many records for his position. But since then, players such as Bruce Smith and J. J. Watt have broken some of those records. As more players pass him on the leaderboards, does White lose some of his edge?

Reggie White is the winner of this defensive line smackdown based on his stats. But many believe Aaron Donald will pass him. Who do you think the winner is? Think it over and make your choice!

Packers fans hold up letters to honor their star defensive lineman. White was one of the NFL's most popular players.

White waves to fans at Lambeau Field in Green Bay, Wisconsin.

SMACKDOWN BREAKDOWN

REGGIE WHITE

Date of birth: December 19, 1961
Height: 6 feet 5 (2 m)
NFL championships: 1
NFL Defensive Player of the Year awards: 2
Pro Bowl games: 13

Stats are accurate through the 2022 NFL season.

AARON DONALD

Date of birth: May 23, 1991
Height: 6 feet 1 (1.9 m)
NFL championships: 1
NFL Defensive Player of the Year awards: 3
Pro Bowl games: 9

GLOSSARY

bench press: to lift a weight by extending the arms upward while lying on a bench

defensive end: a player who plays at the end of the defensive line

defensive tackle: a player who plays in the middle of the defensive line

draft: when teams take turns choosing new players

end zone: the scoring area at each end of the field

fumble: when a football player loses hold of the ball while handling or running with it

interception: a pass caught by the other team that results in a change in possession

NFC: short for National Football Conference, one of two conferences that make up the NFL

prospect: a player who is likely to succeed at a higher level of play

sack: to tackle the quarterback for a loss of yards

scholarship: money that a school or another group gives to students to help pay for their education

LEARN MORE

American Football Facts for Kids
https://kids.kiddle.co/American_football

Graves, Will. *GOATs of Football*. North Mankato, MN: SportsZone, 2022.

Hill, Christina. *Aaron Donald*. Minneapolis: Lerner Publications, 2022.

Jankowski, Matthew. *The Greatest Football Players of All Time*. New York: Gareth Stevens, 2020.

NFL
NFL.com

Sports Illustrated Kids: Football
https://www.sikids.com/football

INDEX

draft, 11

fumble, 16, 20, 23

interception, 16, 21

NFC Championship Game, 16
NFL Defensive Player of the Year, 4, 21, 23
NFL Defensive Rookie of the Year, 12, 15
NFL 100 All-Time Team, 21

playoffs, 16, 18
Pro Bowl, 4, 15, 19
Pro Football Hall of Fame, 4, 21, 23

sack, 4–6, 8–9, 11–13, 15–16, 20, 23, 25
Super Bowl, 4–6, 14, 16, 18

University of Pittsburgh, 11
University of Tennessee, 9

PHOTO ACKNOWLEDGMENTS

Image credits: Lutz Bongarts/Bongarts/Getty Images, p. 4; Cooper Neill/Getty Images, p. 5; MaximilianHaupt/picture alliance/Getty Images, p. 6; Robert Gauthier/Los Angeles Times/Getty Images, p. 7; AP Photo/Joe Holloway Jr., p. 8; AP Photo/Athlon Sports, p. 9; Kevin C. Cox/Getty Images, p. 10; Dilip Vishwanat/Getty Images, p. 11; George Gojkovich/Getty Images, pp. 12, 13; Focus on Sport/Getty Images, pp. 14, 28; Christian Petersen/Getty Images, p. 15; Michael Owens/Getty Images, pp. 17, 18, 25; Rob Brown/Getty Images, p. 19; AP Photo/Mitchell B. Reibel, p. 20; Jay Laprete/Bloomberg/Getty Images, p. 21; Steph Chambers/Getty Images, p. 22; AP Photo/Michael Zorn/Invision for NFL, p. 23; Ronald Martinez/Getty Images, p. 24; Streeter Lecka/Getty Images, p. 26; John Biever/Icon Sportswire/Getty Images, p. 27; Keith Birmingham/MediaNews Group/Pasadena Star-News/Getty Images, p. 29.

Cover: csm/Alamy Stock Photo, (Aaron Donald); AP Photo/ Al Messerschmidt, (Reggie White).